T0207561

THE ART OF EFFECTIVE PUBLIC SPEAKING

THE ART OF EFFECTIVE PUBLIC SPEAKING

Stand Up and Speak Up

RITA CORRAY

Library of Congress Control Number:		2019911244
ISBN:	Hardcover	978-1-7960-5059-2
	Softcover	978-1-7960-5058-5
	eBook	978-1-7960-5057-8

Print information available on the last page.

Rev. date: 09/26/2019

To order additional copies of this book, contact:
Xlibris
1-888-795-4274
www.Xlibris.com
Orders@Xlibris.com
800168

CONTENTS

ACKNOWLEDGEMENTS

I would like to express my heartfelt thanks and gratitude to many people who came into my life and impacted, supported and mentored me.

1. Toastmasters International
2. NAWEM
3. My Church, Metro Tabernacle
4. Mustafa from Bank Negara
5. To my dearly departed parents, Sonny and Girly Corray for loving me and for highlighting the finer principles and values in life.
6. To my dear Sister Amanda Graves who had always supported me, emotionally, spiritually and was always there for me during my good and tiring times, anyone could ever hope to have, for her unfailing love and loyalty. For also spending long hours editing my book.
7. To my Teachers, bosses, friends, relatives and associates who had contributed to my growth over the years.
8. To my dear friend, Patricia Yap from BERJAYA who had always being a source of strength and walking through our leadership journey in Toastmasters together helping Royale Premier Toastmasters Club, BERJAYA University College Toastmasters Club and NAWEM Toastmasters Club. We have together impacted and inspired many people to become better leaders and communicators. Thanks for timely feedback, sharing of leadership experience and editorial suggestions to my book.

9. Lastly, to my husband Bob and my beautiful children, Crystal, Rueben and Ruth for adding special meaning to my life. Thank you Ruth for reviewing and editing my book. This book is specially dedicated to you Ruth, for following my footsteps to learn the ropes of Public Speaking and Writing and putting into practice what I have taught you. I am so proud of you.

PREFACE

The book "Art of Public Speaking" is a profoundly helpful and insightful book giving key components with practical pragmatic ideas on Public Speaking. The ability to speak confidently and well is a talent which is universally admired and envied. The ability to hold an audience, to be heard by those who matter is a crucial skill at any age.

With my professional approach, with many years of Teaching, Training and Coaching people, I wish to offer tips, new hope to anyone seeking to grow and develop their journey in Public Speaking. I am deeply grateful for being able to teach, engage, challenge and inspire people. This is the privilege of the platform.

I have painstakingly gathered through countless years of experience and materials which had significantly broadened and deepened my knowledge and understanding of my first book.

The Journey of a Speaker and having the privilege of the Platform as a Speaker, there is no finishing line. Each moment is a progression of the journey that needs to be celebrated. It is just not the destination but the journey that truly matters.

The fruits of your future success depends on a clear view of where you want to go. As a Speaker, stay committed to developing your own personal vision. Your vision carries the seeds of your future successes. Start planting your seeds now. The triumph is not in the trophy – it is in the striving to do our best.

Every activity of our lives is communication of a sort, but it is through speech that we assert our distinctiveness from other forms of life. We have the gift of verbal communication, our purpose as a human being and it is through the quality of our speech that we best express our own individuality, our essence. When we are unable to say clearly what we mean, due to nervousness, timidity or foggy thought processes, our personality is blocked off, dimmed out and misunderstood.

I have spent nearly all my life helping people get rid of their fears and develop courage and confidence. There were many stories and miracles that have taken place in my classes. I strongly believe that if you follow the directions and suggestions you find in this book. You will definitely have more self-confidence and a deeper sense of personal fulfillment.

INTRODUCTION

An old English proverb says *"Talk is Cheap"*. Whoever coined that phrase obviously did not anticipate the latter part of the twentieth century. Nowadays, talk is expensive.

Congratulations for choosing to read this book. To embark on this journey of transforming yourself to be an Effective Speaker. Building your confidence and learning it step by step to achieve your goals. Whether your goal is to entertain, inform, persuade or to motivate the audience this book should serve you with valuable lessons in Public Speaking, whatever your reasons or goals, in speaking your mind will grow. And you'll experience your world at a deeper, more stimulating level than you even thought possible.

"Once Bitten, Twice Shy" you may have had bad past experiences and labeled as shy or lack of confidence. This book has special strategies specially designed to break the cycle of habitual shyness.

The author has thoroughly enjoyed reading books all her life and this has greatly helped her in compiling the book. Her only desire is to share with you what she has learnt from her life-time's study. It will give her immense pleasure to know that you have benefited from it.

Getting audience attention through audience participation, making the audience a "partner to the talk" by identifying their expectations, speaking to their needs, and using our own background and experiences to connect with them. The importance of using concrete, familiar words to create vivid pictures to capture your audience attention and to drive our point home.

I was deeply inspired by the Zen proverb, "When the student is ready, the teacher will appear." Listen to your inner voice, and you will grow and be guided along a path to greater happiness and fulfilment. If you aspire to be a better or professional speaker, this book has all the answers for you.

Imagine yourself as a totally confident and comfortable person standing before your audience.

Rita had laid the foundation and groundwork by providing tips on

1. How to conquer the main barrier to effective speaking.
2. Visualization Techniques. How to approach ever step in the preparation of successful speech.
3. Structuring Your Speech
4. Style and Delivery
5. How to gain an audience's commitment with a "call-to-action".

LEARNING OBJECTIVES

At the end of the Workshop you will be able to:

Objectives

- create confidence in making persuasive presentations
- understand the principles of clear and effective communication
- know how to plan and prepare a professional presentation
- learn and practice proven techniques of up-front speaking skills
- learn and practice the skills of handling questions
- learn and practice the skills of developing rapport with audience
- learn and practice the techniques of starting well and finishing
- project a better image of themselves and the organization
- improve proficiency in standard spoken English

WHAT IS PUBIC SPEAKING?

What is public speaking?

Public Speaking is about delivering your Speech in Public. It is more formal and highly structured. Every Speaker is given a time limit to complete their Speech. It is more formal and it is addressed to a large audience. A mentor can help you and with practice you can acquire the necessary skills required to be a great Speaker.

Public speaking is one of the biggest fear faced by most human beings in their lives.

This is because every time that person try to express their ideas, present their thoughts, or sell their services, they are facing their biggest fear, which is being rejected, are not being liked.

By becoming a confident and capable public speaker you instantly put yourself above many other people who refuse to stand up and speak.

It is a presentation that's given live or face to face before an audience.

Public speeches can cover a wide variety of different topics. The goal of the speech may be to

- Educate
- Entertain or
- Influence the listeners.

Electronic slideshows are used t as visual aids to supplement the speech and make it more interesting to the listeners. It means to speak to a crowd in public, usually it is regarding a certain subject like for example, "English Communication in the Workplace" it is something related to work you give a speech to give people facts and information in a way that gives them the knowledge but keeps them interested.

In this book, we share some approaches, different experiences, practical and simple tools and honest and individual feedback to help and guide you to become a better speaker. Seize every opportunity to practice.

As a result, each reader can gain more confidence, become more assertive, increase their influencing skill and have a successful presence when speaking, presenting or interacting with groups.

Public speaking is a skill that is best mastered through continuous practice.

A talkative person may not be able to give the best speech. To give a great speech, one must first understand the type of speech one is expected to give and should prepare along those lines. A good Public Speaker is one who understands the needs of the audience and is flexible enough to adopt changes that may arise even while delivering the speech.

<u>WHY IS PUBIC SPEAKING IMPORTANT?</u>

Public Speaking is important because one day it will certainly touch you in your life.

When it does, you want to be ready and present yourself skillfully. Public Speaking is important for your career success or for people in businesses to get their message across to customers and it is important to master the skills of Public Speaking.

By becoming a confident and capable public speaker you instantly put yourself above many other people who refuse to stand up and speak. Public speaking will improve you communication skill, your leadership skill, your confidence and your ability to read and understand people.

Types of Public Speaking Speeches

There are many types and varieties of Public Speaking Speeches. We need to address the audience in a structured manner to suit their needs. The purpose of the speech is to

- To Inform
- To Persuasive
- Special Occasion
- To Entertain
- Demonstrative
- Motivation
- Entertaining

- Introducing Speakers
- Presenting or Accepting Awards

Speaking to Inform

This type of public speaking **focuses on explaining a concept or idea to convey knowledge effectively to the audience.**

Speaking to inform occurs in a wide range of everyday situations. Informative speakers tend to focus on specific subject matter, such as people, events, places, stories using an informative approach.

Speaking to Persuade

Persuasive speaking has always been among the most challenging of rhetorical exercises. This is the bread and butter of Public Speaking. It's downright difficult to convince an audience to believe something, agreeing with your viewpoint or to take a particular action.

When you give a persuasive speech, it's important to prevent a disconnect between what you say and what the audience needs to hear. The ability to persuade, influence and build consensus is the most important skill that you can have in workplace. How do make yourself more persuasive? I's not easy and it requires constant attention and preparation. In Persuasive communication if you wish to be more persuasive then you must add these skills to your toolbox. The five words that make you more persuasive are clarity, brevity, context, impact and value.

Demonstrative speeches

Demonstrative speeches are ones **where the speaker performs actions, and clearly explains those actions in the process.**

The idea is to engage the audience in both verbal and non-verbal communicational methods. By doing so, the speaker has a better chance to get the message across to the audience.

Have you ever witnessed a cheesy product commercial? You know, the ones where the host goes on and on about some product and shows you all the features?

Science demonstrations and role playing are types of demonstrative speaking.

Motivational

A motivational public speaker will inspire and uplift the audience using stories, anecdotes and illustrations in his/her speech.

Entertaining

After dinner speeches are normally to entertain the guests and they usually have a lighter touch . Humor is added to stimulate the audience.

There are many ways to Entertain an audience. You can:

- tell jokes
- tell funny stories
- dramatize an anecdote
- tell a scary story

Entertaining Speeches are used during weddings, or giving an Acceptance Speech or at a Seminar to entertain or captivate the audience when delivering a speech. The purpose is to amuse or arouse the audience emotionally where they add Humor and Drama to stir them emotionally and make them laugh.

Introducing A Speaker

The purpose of a speech of introduction is to focus attention on the main speaker, not on the person making the introduction. It should be about two or three minutes.

Speeches Of Acceptance

The purpose of an acceptance speech is to give thanks for a gift or an award for a gift or an award. You should thank the people who are bestowing the award and you should recognize the people who helped you gain it. The three major traits of a good acceptance speech are brevity, humility and graciousness.

YOUR SPEAKING JOURNEY

A Thousand-mile Journey Starts With One Small Step

The mountain of learning has no peak but climbing it has its rewards. Life is a building process. What you do today affects what you will have tomorrow. The effort you put in today does make a difference. If you want to be a great Speaker or Trainer you must start with a DREAM.

Do you Dare to Dream Big. A Dream will remain a Dream until someone starts weaving it. "From fragmented ideas and disjointed thoughts, we began the process of weaving our Dreams.

Dare to Dream

A dream does many things for us.
A Dream Gives Us Direction
A Dream increases our Potential
A Dream Adds Value to our Work
A Dream predicts our futures.

We have a Dream, we are not just spectators sitting back hoping that everything turns out right. We are taking an active part in shaping the purpose and meaning of our lives.

And the winds of change do not simply blow us here and there.

How Do We Weave Our Dreams?

We talk all the ideas
Sifted through many big ideas
We threaded every single thought
Stringing ideas and tied in petty knots
Working through rules and regulations
We remembered to follow instructions

Interfacing colored yard with loom
Stitch by stitch our fingers moved
Needling through our handiwork
making sure it was collective teamwork
weaving our fine fabric
Knowing our dream would soon come true

Our Dreams when pursued, is the most likely predictor of our future,
that doesn't mean we have any quarters, but it does increase our chances
for success tremendously.
Dare to dream and act on that Dream. Dream to be a better Speaker
and Communicator.

IGNITE YOUR PURPOSE AND PASSION

"Passion is energy. Feel the power that comes from focusing on what excites you."- Oprah Winfrey

Passion is the fire that fuels our energy and opens us up to opportunities and the excitement for life. It burns within us about what we do in our life, our work Passion comes when you are being yourself and doing what comes naturally to you. **When what you do is in alignment with who you are, you get energy from doing it.** I feel very happy that I have found my passion and I'm living it every single day. And let me tell you –it is so incredibly fabulous to be able to make a living doing what you love!!! True happiness comes when you do what you are most passionate about.

Passion vs. Purpose

passion – noun 1. A strong and barely controllable emotion.

purpose – noun 1. The reason for which something is done or created or for which something exists.

Passion and purpose go hand in hand. When you discover your purpose, you will normally find it's something you're tremendously passionate about." — **Steve Pavlina,**

Enthusiasm is one of the most powerful engines of success. When you do a thing, do it with all your might. Put your whole soul into it. Stamp it with your own personality. Be active, be energetic and faithful, and you will accomplish your object. Nothing great was ever achieved without enthusiasm." — **Ralph Waldo Emerson**

QUOTES

BORN TO WIN

What Lies Behind Us
And What Lies Before Us
Are Tiny Matters Compared To
What Lies Within Us

By Oliver Wedell Holmes

Yesterday Is Gone
Tomorrow Is But A Dream
Today Is A Gift
That Is Why
It Is Called "The Present"

By Peter Masang

"Some See Things
As They Are And Ask Why
But I See Things
As They Never Were
And Ask Why Not?

Robert Kennedy

"You Can't Build A Reputation On
What You Are Going To Do"

Henry Ford

I Am Only One
But Still I Am One
I Cannot Do Everything
But Still I Can Do Something
I will Not Refuse To Do The
Something I Can Do

Helen Killier

OVERCOMING NERVOUSNESS/SHYNESS

"The way to develop Self-Confidence is to do the things you fear"
By Willam Jennings Bry'an

Research shows that 76% of experienced speakers have stage fright before being on stage. The secret is to rehearse the speech until it is just right.

Conquering Your Fear is to control the "Butterflies". Here are some tips on how to control the "Butterflies".

1. Get to know the audience – greet or chat with the audience beforehand. It's easier to speak to friends than strangers.
2. Know your material – Increased nervousness is due to poor preparation.
3. Relax your body by stretching and breathing to ease the tension.
4. Visualize giving your speech from start to finish. By visualizing success, you are more likely to be successful.
5. Gain experience – experience builds confidence, which is the key to effective Public Speaking.
6. Don't apologize – by mentioning your nervousness or apologizing, you'll only alerting the audience's attention to mistakes which they might otherwise not be aware of.
7. Turn nervousness into positive energy.
8. Pick a speech topic you truly like or know and then prepare it.
9. Think positively
10. Take a couple of deep breaths.

11. Work on your introduction
12. Make eye contact with your audience
13. Use visual aids

One of the most inhibiting obstacles to personal growth is the feeling of awkwardness that affects many of us when we feel uncomfortable and tongue-tied in unfamiliar surroundings. This feeling of shyness exists at different levels of severity in all of us.

Shyness is a universal social obstacle, experienced by many people. Fumbling for the right words, inability to socialize to mix freely among strangers, to relax and enjoy new friends, to say the right things at the right time, can develop into limitations that can stunt our personal enjoyment of life and inhibit our self-confidence.

It is worthwhile to make an effort to overcome shyness, mainly because it is a major obstacle to personal growth. If you can overcome shyness, you will notice a different world. You will enjoy relationships and opportunities will open up for you and you will be a much happier person.

Shyness is basically caused by feelings of insecurity and low self-worth. It is the result of a lack of confidence in ourselves, and comes from a belief that we are not good enough. Some quotations

You Can, If You Think You Can
If You Think, You Are Beaten, You Are!
If You Think, You Dare Not...You Won't!
Success Begins With Your Own Will,
It's All In Your State of Mind
Life's Battles Are Not Always Won
By Those Who Are Stronger Or Faster
And Stronger or Faster
The Person Who Wins Is The Person Who Thinks
He Can!

The moment you are in Tension
You will lose your Attention
Ten you are in total Confusion
And you'll feel Irritation
Then you'll spoil personal Relation
Ultimately, you won't get Cooperation
Then you'll make things Complication
Then your BP may also rise Caution
And you may have to take Medication
Instead, understand the Situation
And try to think about the Solution
Many problems will be solved by Discussion
Which will work out better in your Profession
Don't think its my free Suggestion
It is only for your Prevention
If you understand my Intention
You'll never come again to Tension!!

Mind and modern problems
By Swami Bodhamayananda

UNDERSTANDING YOUR AUDIENCE

Public Speaking is audience centered. It is crucial that you interact with the people you are addressing. Selecting your topic, establishing your purpose and narrowing the topic require consideration of your audience. If you do not adapt to your listeners, you will probably not be an effective Speaker.

When you begin your audience analysis, you will want to ask the following questions.

- ➢ Age
- ➢ Educational Level
- ➢ Ethnic Composition
- ➢ Language Proficiency
- ➢ Professional Composition
- ➢ Class or Social Status
- ➢ Level of Competence

It is also useful to divide audience members into psychological groups on the basis of fundamental beliefs, attitudes and values. This is especially important if you intend to influence your listeners' thinking.

USING 4 P'S – TO A POWERFUL PRESENTATION

- Plan
- Prepare
- Practice
- Present

'THE 1ST 'P' - PLANNING YOUR SPEECH

THE PURPOSE OF THE SPEECH

- Decide what you wish to speak about
- Decide what is the primary purpose of the speech
- Do you wish to
  - Instruct and inform
  - Convince, persuade, influence or motivate or
- Amuse and entertain What are
  you trying to achieve?
  What are the objectives of your speech
  Know your audience
  Know the venue

SELECTING A TOPIC

The first step in speechmaking is choosing a topic. After deciding what to talk about, narrow it down to a specific subject that you are familiar with. The Topic chosen must

> ➤ Must be timely and relevant to your audience.
> ➤ Must be one that you can speak with some degree of authority
> ➤ Must be one which you can deliver with enthusiasm and conviction.

Determine your purpose in giving this talk. What specific point you want imprinted in your audience's mind?

In your Speech do you want to

> ➤ Inform / Explain?
> ➤ Persuade / Convince?
> ➤ Entertain / Humor?
> ➤ Motivate / Inspire?

Once you understand what you want to say and who your audience is, you must collect some substantive materials to fill out and support your ideas. Organize your ideas into a logical sequence.

'THE 2ND 'P' - PREPARING YOUR SPEECH

Preparing a speech is a little like constructing a jigsaw puzzle? You have to plan and gather materials. The better you know your material the less anxious you'll be about presenting it. There are a number of ways to source for information. The following are some tips.

- Using your own knowledge and experience
- Interviewing
- Writing for Information
- Searching the Internet
- Doing Library Research
- Newspaper
- Television

There are many resources available if you take advantage of them. If you start early you will ease the tension of completing the assignment. Instead of sweating under intense time pressure, you can work at your convenience. It helps avoid the pitfalls that come from procrastinating. It also gives you plenty of time to think about what you find.

Background Information

You can obtain background information from the library. The reference section puts a wealth of information at your fingertips. It contains encyclopedias, yearbooks, dictionaries, biographical aids, atlases, and periodical indexes.

Suppose you want to find a particular piece of factual information (such as the number of deaths caused by drunk drivers in Malaysia last year. You can find it in the Internet or research session in the library.

Newspapers are invaluable for research on many topics, historical as well as current issues of several newspapers are now indexed way back in the 50's, Use statistics to quantify our ideas. Use statistics sparingly. Nothing puts an audience to sleep faster than a speech cluttered with numbers from beginning to end. Insert statistics only when they are needed, and then make sure they are easy to grasp.

<u>BEGINNING THE SPEECH</u>

First Impressions are important. A poor beginning may so distract or alienate listeners that the speaker can never fully recover. In most speeches you need to accomplish the following:

- Get the Attention and Interest of your audience.
- Reveal the topic of your speech
- Establish your credibility and good will
- Preview the body of the speech.

Getting the initial attention of your audience is usually easy to do – even before you utter a single word. After you are introduced and step to the lectern, your audience will normally give you their attention. If they don't, merely wait patiently. Look directly at the audience without saying a word. In a few moments all talking and physical commotion will stop. Your listeners will be attentive. You will be ready to start speaking.

Keeping the attention of your audience once you start talking is more difficult. Here are the methods used most often.

Relate the topic to the Audience. People pay attention to things that affect them directly. If you can relate the topic to your listeners, they are much more likely to be interested in it.

State the importance of your topic. Tell your audience why they should think so too.

Arouse the curiosity of the audience. People are curious. One way to draw them into your speech is with a series of statements that progressively whet their curiosity about the subject of the speech.

Asking a rhetorical question is another way to get your listeners thinking about your speech. Sometimes a single question will do. Example: "Do you remember your first Date?"

Begin with a quotation is another way to arouse the interest of your audience is to start with an attention-getting quotation. You might choose your quotation from the words of a famous speaker or politician, from Shakespeare, from the Bible or even from a poem or song.

Tell a story. We all enjoy stories especially if they are amusing, dramatic, or suspenseful. To work well as introductions, they should also be clearly relevant to the main point of the speech. Stories are perhaps the most effective way to begin a speech.

Establish credibility and good will is important. Credibility is mostly a matter of being qualified to speak on a given topic. As being perceived as qualified by your listeners.

Tips for Preparing the Introduction

1. Keep the introduction relatively brief. Under normal circumstances it should not constitute more than about 10 to 20 percent of your speech.
2. Be on the lookout for possible introductory materials as you do your research. File them with your notes, so they will be handy when you are ready for them.
3. Be creative in devising your introduction. Experiment with two or three different openings and choose the one that seems most likely to get the audience interested in your speech.
4. Don't worry about the exact wording of your introduction until you have finished preparing the body of the speech. After you have determined your main points, it will be much easier to make final decisions about how to begin the speech.
5. Work out your introduction in detail. Practice the introduction over and over until you can deliver it smoothly from a minimum of notes and with strong eye contact. This will get your speech off to a good start and give you a big boost of confidence.

OPENING REMARKS

1. Welcome and thank you for the opportunity to share.
2. Going to have a good time together.
3. Don't have to be solemn to be serious – have some fun.
4. Get relaxed and comfortable – make yourself at home.

5. Have a coffee whenever you feel like it – no formality.
6. Housekeeping info: Timings, breaks, lunch, finish time, telephone, toilets etc

ENDING A SPEECH

"Great is the art of beginning" said Longfellow, "but greater is the art is of ending the speech" Many a speaker has marred an otherwise fine speech by a long-winded, silly conclusion. Your closing remarks are your last chance to drive home your ideas. Moreover, your final impression will probably linger in your listeners' minds. Thus you need to craft your conclusion with as much care as your introduction.

You should signal the end of the speech by letting your audience know you are going to stop soon. Don't end your speech by concluding abruptly that you are taken by surprise.

How do you let an audience know your speech is ending? One way is through what you say.

"In conclusion"
"One last thought"
"In Closing"
"My purpose has been"
"Let me end by saying"

Summarize your speech by restating the main points is the easiest way to end a speech. The value of a summary is that it explicitly restates the central idea and main points one last time.

You could either end with a quotation. A quotation is one of the most common and effective devices to conclude a speech. The closing quotation is particularly good because its urgency is exactly suited to the speech.

An excellent way to give your speech psychological unity is to conclude by referring to ideas in the introduction. This is an easy technique to use, and it may give your speech an extra touch of class.

Summarizing the speech, ending with a quotation, making a dramatic statement, referring to the introduction, all these techniques can be used separately.

A successful talk is a little miracle—people see the world differently afterward. Conceptualizing and framing what you want to say is the most vital part of preparation.

ORGANIZING YOUR SPEECH

Your speech should be structured into 3 distinct parts – Introduction/ Opening, Body and Conclusion. Clear organization is vital to speechmaking. Listeners demand coherence. They get only one chance to grasp a speaker's ideas, and they have litter patience for Speakers who ramble aimlessly from one idea to another.

A well organized speech will enhance your credibility and make it easier for the audience to understand your message. It also helps you to command attention and interest and to inspire the confidence of your audience. With good organization your ideas will be easy to follow and understand. They will flow naturally and logically, and will build to a persuasive climax.

Early in your preparation you may want to make a rough sketch of the points you wish to include in your speech.

<u>PLANNING SHEET</u>

SUBJECT/TOPIC   :

OBJECTIVES   :

INTRODUCTION   :

BODY   :

RECOMMENDATION   :

CONCLUSION   :

APPENDIX   :

'THE 3TH 'P' - PRACTICE YOUR SPEECH

PRACTICE, PRACTICE, PRACTICE There's an interesting paradox in Public Speaking. If you haven't practiced, you will appear nervous. But if you have practiced until it is second nature to say these words with expression, gestures, emphasis, and passion, you will appear spontaneous, as if you are speaking "off the cuff".

Practice until you are familiar with the speech. Practice helps to reduce nervousness.

Practice:

1. **In front of family**
2. **To gain feedback**
3. **Using a tape recorder**
4. **A strong opening**
5. **To ensure logical flow**
6. **Credible evidence**
7. **To identify distracting mannerisms**

To ensure your speech is within the allocated time period. 9.

Remember,

Giving a speech without adequate practice is like taking bread out of the oven before it is fully cooked.

'THE 4TH 'P' - PRESENTATION

DELIVERY

Delivery includes the presenter's style and his or her ability in knowing how to use verbal and nonverbal communication, questioning and reinforcement, group interaction, and the appropriate use of humor. Some guidelines to make your presentation a winner include:

- Keep your presentation within or under the allotted time.
- Make sure you have enough breaks.
- Avoid last-minute emergencies
- Don't rush
- Don't allow yourself to be angry, frustrated or annoyed with anyone or anything.
- Arrive early
- Check out the room, stage and equipment
- Don't be demanding, be flexible
- Socialize
- Smile a lot! – Keep you from looking tense
- Maintain eye contact with your audience throughout your presentation.
- Show enthusiasm.
- Deliver presentations in your own style.
- Keep the audience's attention.

DELIVERY - THE CRITICAL FIRST THIRTY MINUTES

Know what you are trying to achieve in the first 30 minutes of the session.

The first 30 minutes (particularly) the first ten) will set the tone and atmosphere for the rest of the session. It should be devoted to:

1. Gaining attention and interest.
2. Developing comfort and rapport.
3. Providing information and expectations
4. Establishing a receptive learning environment.

When people enter a strange room, especially with a group of strangers in it, they feel tentative, even a little nervous. Therefore, greet them at the door with a welcoming smile as they come in. Look pleased to see them. Introduce yourself, show them where they are supposed to sit, introduce them to at least two other people, and invite them to have a coffee before the session begins. Make them feel at home.

Always start on time and always finish on time. Keep your promises.

Concentrate on the happy faces. In the early part of the session, it pays to concentrate on the happy faces in the group, not the 'scowlers' This helps with your confidence and comfort which is critical in those few opening minutes.

BODY LANGUAGE

What's your Body Telling You?

Body Language is using Gestures, Poses, Movements, Facial Expressions that a person uses to communicate. The following are how Body Language is used:

7% Verbal (Words)
38% Vocal (Intonation, Pitch and Pauses)
55% Non Verbal (Body Language)

There are Five types of Body Language

- Eye Contact
- Facial Expression
- Gestures
- Posture and Stance
- Space

Eyes

Eyes are the window of your Soul. Eyes are so transparent that through them one sees the soul.

Look at a person in the Eye when you Speak to them.

Facial Expressions

Can Your Face Speak?

- Happiness
- Sadness
- Displeasure
- Anger
- Fear
- Interest

Consider your body language and the message that it conveys.

- Practice standing with a relaxed upright posture.
- Place your hands at your sides or clasped in front of you, unless you are making a gesture to emphasize a point.
- Become aware of your facial expressions as well; they should match the message you are delivering. If you're giving an upbeat speech, try to be relaxed

2. Using space.

As a Speaker the space on the stage is yours and maximize the space by the way you stand, move and speak in public.

You can use different parts of the stage. For example, you can move to the center of the stage, pause, and deliver your point.

Part of being a successful speaker is to position yourself correctly in front of an audience. Don't out stage yourself. Your strongest position is center stage. Return to this position after using the flipchart. Ty to face the audience, as this is your strongest body position.

Hand Gestures

Public Speakers must have a vast repertoire of graceful hand gestures that can add impact to a speech. It should appear natural and spontaneous, to help clarify or reinforce your ideas and be suited to the audience and occasion. Your gestures must match your message. You can use them to emphasize a point in your speech. The primary rule is that whatever gestures you make should not draw attention to themselves and distract from your message. Examples of hand gestures, when you open your palms, it communicates that you are open, honest and can be trusted. To signal transitions, you can use your fingers to reinforce the first, second, and third points.

THE POWER OF THE SPEAKER'S VOICE

A golden voice is certainly an asset. And it will definitely affect the success of your speeches. The aspects of voice you should work on are the volume, pitch, rate, pauses, variety, pronunciation and articulation.

The moment you open your mouth to speak, you are going to disclose something about yourself. How you phrase your question, give an opinion and your manner of speech reveal almost all there is to know about you. So think before you speak. Never open your mouth before you form that thought. If you speak softly, you are judged to be shy, if you speak loudly, you are aggressive, if you speak in a moderate tone, you are therefore a confident speaker.

Your voice is the link between you and to your listeners. It is the primary medium for conveying your message. A good speaking voice has several qualities. It is

- ➢ Pleasant - A friendly tone
- ➢ Natural - Natural voice of the speaker
- ➢ Forceful - conveying vitality and Energy
- ➢ Expressive - demonstrating various shades meaning
- ➢ Easily heard - as a result of proper volume

Your Speaking Voice

If the eyes are the windows of the soul, the voice is the front door. Your voice must be loud enough to be heard, it will depend on whether you are addressing a small group or large crowd and you need to project your voice accordingly.

Your voice is a vital part of Public Speaking. Your voice carries your ideas to your listeners and it is important to hear when you speak. When you mumble and your voice trembles, or has no expression, your listeners may think that you are an uninteresting person and very nervous.

Do you know that your voice is like a yardstick? People use I to measure and judge your capabilities. It is important for you to understand how your voice works. You must know how to manage the tone, the volume, the pitch, vocal variety, diction and clarity.

The elements of vocal quality are as follows:

- Is loud enough
- Has an adequate and varied rate of speech
- Uses clear diction
- Has a pleasant pitch
- Has good phrasing.
- Uses frequent pauses
- Makes a variety of sound

Unleash the Power of your voice by practicing your voice and with practical voice exercises you'll quickly will learn to speak with more confidence, clarity and conviction. Find a voice coach to assist you.

You voice coaching will also:

- Help control your nerves.
- Focus your thoughts and
- Improve how you come across to your audience.

Vocal Variety

Just as variety is the spice of life, so is it the spice of Public Speaking. When giving a speech, you should modulate your voice to convey your ideas and feelings. Varying your voice plays a very significant role and is a fundamental part of Public Speaking.

Some Tips and Pointers you should work to control your voice and make it sound better are volume, pitch, rate, pauses, variety, pronunciation and articulation.

Voice Techniques

1. Inflexion - Variation in Speed
2. Pitch and Volume
3. Clear Diction and Pitch
4. Make use of the Pause
5. Avoid Verbal Drags – eg "ahs, wanna, you know, um

Volume

Today, we are blessed with Technology, we can use the microphone if we have a soft voice. But sometimes these gadgets are not available in the classroom.

You adjust your voice according to the setting of the room. You must have your own built-in microphone to amplify the sound produced.

Most of the time we speak without a microphone. You have to adjust your voice to the size of the audience, and the level of background noise.

Rate

Rate refers to the speed at which a person speaks. Malaysians usually speak at a rate between 20 and 150 words per minute.

The best rate of speech depends on several things

The vocal, attributes of the speaker, the mood, the composition of the audience and the nature of the occasion.

Pitch

Pitch is the highness or lowness of the speaker's voice. The faster sound waves vibrate, the higher their pitch; the slower they vibrate, the lower their pitch.

Changes in pitch are known as inflections. They give your voice luster, warmth and vitality.

Pitch tells your listeners how you feel about what you are saying. Speaking at too high a pitch makes the voice sound piercing and metallic.

Good Speakers vary the pitch of their voices to convey emotion and conviction. **Pause between ideas** to give the audience time to digest what you are saying.

Your voice should be expressive, showing a wide range of emotion. An expressive voice adds more meaning to the words you use, enhances your message and adds interest for your audience. You must develop a lively, expressive voice by doing every speech as an opportunity to share your ideas, your sense of conviction and spark it with energy.

Pronunciation

Good English pronunciation is challenging because the English Language is difficult to pronounce. Pronunciation is the way a word is said. It requires knowledge. You must know how to say each sound in a word, which part of a word is stressed.

We all mispronounce words very often and it may cause listeners to make negative judgements about your personality, intelligence, competence and integrity. **Carefully articulate and pronounce your words**. A mumbling Public Speaker is hard to understand. Some people mix up sounds when they are talking.

EXPLOITING VISUAL AIDS

Visual aids offer several advantages. As the old saying tells us, *"A picture is worth a thousand words"*. People find a speaker's message more interesting, grasp it more easily and retain it longer when it is presented visually as well as verbally. By using visual aids in your speeches, you often will make it easier for listeners to understand exactly what you are trying to communicate. Your message is clearer by showing the object.

Research has shown that we take in more information from seeing than listening in the ratio of 75% sight and 25% hearing.

Visual Aids should enhance, dramatize and clarify the information you are presenting – not take away from it. Use them for emphasis and explanation. When prepared and presented well, they act as triggers to stimulate learning and memory recall.

Some Tips on Visual Aids:

Attract and hold attention
Keep your visuals simple
Be Creative with your visuals.
Brighten them up with colors
Use the 7 x 7 rule for written visuals Use acronyms as
coat hangers' for the memory
Make graphs as simple as possible

Kinds of Visual Aids

1. Objects or equipment's
2. Models
3. Photographs
4. Drawings
5. Graphs
6. Charts
7. Slides
8. PowerPoint slides
9. Flip Charts

WORDS HAVE POWER

**Words can inspire. And words can destroy.
Choose your Words well.**

"Your words have power. Speak words that are kind, loving, positive, uplifting, encouraging, and life-giving." -Unknown

The words you write or speak to others can leave a huge impact and create a lasting memory—either good or bad—so it's super important to choose them wisely. Words can make or break a relationship and your choice of words and the way you express yourself can accelerate or kill your career. The words you write or speak to others can leave a huge impact and create a lasting memory—either good or bad—so it's super important to choose them wisely. Words can make or break a relationship and your choice of words and the way you express yourself can accelerate or kill your career.

"If we understood the power of our thoughts, we would guard them more closely. If we understood the awesome power of our words, we would prefer silence to almost anything negative. In our thoughts and words, we create our own weaknesses and our own strengths. Our limitations and joys begin in our hearts. We can always replace negative with positive." -Betty Eadie

The English Language is one of the richest in the world. It is also the largest and has 600,000 words. With almost 1 million words in the

English Language at their disposal, smart leaders realize they must choose words that will significantly determine the impact of their message.

After all, words form internal representations in the mind(s) of their listeners. The ultimate measure of a presentation's effectiveness is whether people pay attention, apply what was said, follow through or take action on the message.

An average person only uses 1,000 to 1,200 words in his lifetime.

Oral Versus Written Language

- Spoken words are a "One Shot" deal
- Once spoken, the words are gone forever
- Must be immediately understandable to the ear.

Clarity

- Use short and simple sentences
- Speak to express, not to impress
- Avoid bombastic words
- Avoid ambiguity. Use words that are specific
- *K.I.S.S "Keep It Short and Simple" or "Keep It Sophisticated and Smarty"*

Words are the building blocks of effective communication. When speaking with words or phrase would you use? The Simplier word or the More sophisticated word?

"Words are the universal currency of humankind," says Anu Garg, CTM, CL, a member of Eastside Toastmasters in Redmond, Washington, and the author of three books on words. "The better we are with them, the better we can be in anything we do."

Be mindful when it comes to your words. A string of some that don't mean much to you, may stick with someone else for a lifetime." -Rachel Wolchin

"Be careful with your words. Once they are said, they can be only forgiven, not forgotten." – Unknown

"Words are free. It's how you use them that may cost you." –Kushand Wizdom

"Raise your words, not your voice. It is rain that grows flowers, not thunder." –Rumi

Words Have Power

Smart leaders don't waste their time trying to convince people. They use these 5 words and phrases in order to penetrate people's unconscious filters and create meaning. All smart leaders focus on them in order to sell the meaning they want people to associate with their vision, product or idea. Effective communication is a science and an art. You can learn it too.

SPEAK OFF-THE-CUFF

There may come a time in our life when someone will tap you on the shoulder and say "How about a few words?" It comes without any warning. The ability to assemble and mobilize one's thoughts and to verbalize it fluently and to speak on the spur of the moment is even more important, in some ways, than the ability to speak only after preparation. For instance, you might be asked unexpectedly for your opinion in a meeting at work, or be prompted to say a few words at a family gathering. Either way it is very useful to be able to start speaking with the knowledge that you can get your point across effectively (and are able to quickly decide what your point should be in the first place!)

Speak Off-The-Cuff Means

The phrase "Off the Cuff" is believed to have originated with waiters who were among the first to use their shirt cuffs as notepads to take orders. The speaker is pictured as hurriedly jotting down notes on his cardboard starched shirt cuff during the meal and delivering them afterwards from arm's length note card.

Impromptu speaking is to speak without preparing a speech but to speak extemporaneously or to render a spoken opinion. Although practicing and delivering prepared speeches can have a profound effect on your confidence and Communication Skill, in the real world you often don't have the luxury of being able to plan what you say in advance.

At home, you could try speaking for a minute or two out loud about something in the news. You might even record yourself speaking and play it back. Listening to the recording – how effective was your mini-speech? Did you have a clear point that was easy to follow or did you ramble?

At Toastmasters, each meeting has a section dedicated to impromptu speaking. During "table topics" members are invited to deliver a short speech on a topic chosen by the evening's "Table Topics Master". This is a great opportunity to practice speaking "off-the-cuff" in a friendly and supportive environment where it really doesn't matter if you mess it up.

"Think on your Feet" or Impromptu speaking is about speaking at random and to get people to learn to think and speak on their feet. It is like a mini speech and you do not have time to prepare the speech. You need to prepare yourself mentally for these situations by conditioning yourself mentally to speak impromptu on all occasions. You are required to think on your part, and thinking is the hardest thing in the world to do.

DEVELOPING GOOD SPEECH HABITS

We humans are creatures of habit, therefore developing good habits should be simple - right! Well, not always. The problem is that we get very comfortable doing things the same way each and every day. We often stick to a daily routine without considering the consequence or effectiveness of it. Why change?

Successful speakers know that speaking is hard work. There's no shortcut to success. Get out there and speak. Share your message. Speak as often as you can. You need to find the only fortune worth finding, your rich, hidden talents. The seeds of GREANESS that God plants inside everyone of us. Ever wonder what makes some speaker super successful? Have you ever sat in an audience in awe of a speaker and pondered "How did she do that?" The answer is through a lot of work. There are some freaks (meant lovingly of course) out there who are natural gifted at speaking, but most of us have to work really hard at it. Patience is bitter, but its fruit is sweet. Follow the following Tips to improve your Speech.

Deliver with Passion. It is important to have passion. It's amazing how catchy enthusiasm can be caught by the people around you. If your voice is expressive and your gestures animated, you will appear confident and passionate.

Enthusiasm - Channel adrenaline into enthusiasm. Control physical stage-fright symptoms by breathing from the diaphragm, you will appear confident and passionate.

Humor – Humor helps when used appropriately

Language – Good grammar improves your credibility

SEVEN GREAT HABITS TO BE A SUCCESSFUL SPEAKER

I got better through speaking more and observing the habits of successful speakers.

Habit #1: Develop A Goal and Purpose For Your Presentation

Writing down a goal is like turning on a switch. Pencil touching paper is like joining two electric wires together to form a path for the flow of electric power. There's nothing like a written down goal to s-t-r-e-t-c-h a man to a BIGGER size. By writing down your goal on paper can you harness your subconscious mind to go to work to realize your goal. If you have no goal, you drift and get nowhere. If you have too any goals, you scatter your energies and get no where

Habit #2: Plan and Prepare

Plans and blueprints are essential to architecture. Think what might happen if you tried to build a house without a floor or blue print. Building your outline for your speech is like a blueprint for your speech. By outlining, you make sure that related items are together, that ideas flow from one to another, that the structure of your speech will "stand Up" and not collapse.

Habit #3: Organize

Organize your message so it flows smoothly. The structure of a speech is very important. There are a few different types of structures you can use. The most common one is

- **Introduction**
- **Body**
- **Conclusion**

The Process

The following format will help you organise your presentation:

- **Outline what you propose to cover**
- **Give the body of the presentation, including facts or statistics where it is relevant to do so**
- **Summarise what you've covered and conclude**
- **Invite questions from the audience**

Another structure you can use is

TRET
T: Topic
R: Reason
E: Examples
T: Topic

By using this TRET you help your audience to remember your message better.

Habit #4: Involve Your Audience

Connect with the Audience – Zero in on your audience's needs, and do your best to satisfy them.

Habit #5: Respect The Time Limit ALWAYS

Pay attention to timing. A good strategy for a presentation is to plan, prepare and practice and present. Ending late is poor planning.

Plan your presentation thoroughly to time and re-emphasise at least three things you want the audience to remember you by. Use visual aids, such as pictures and table graphs. Rehearse, rehearse. Anticipate the questions you might be asked based on the content of your presentation. Think through the answers you might give

Habit #6: Show Up Early

Come early. Relax and prepare yourself physically and mentally for the presentation. Get all the equipment, notes ready before the audience arrive.

Habit #7: Practice

Practice - Practice out loud saying the speech differently each time you repeat it.

A Chinese saying by Confucius,

**If I Hear
I Forget
If I See
I Remember
If I Practice
I Make It My Own**

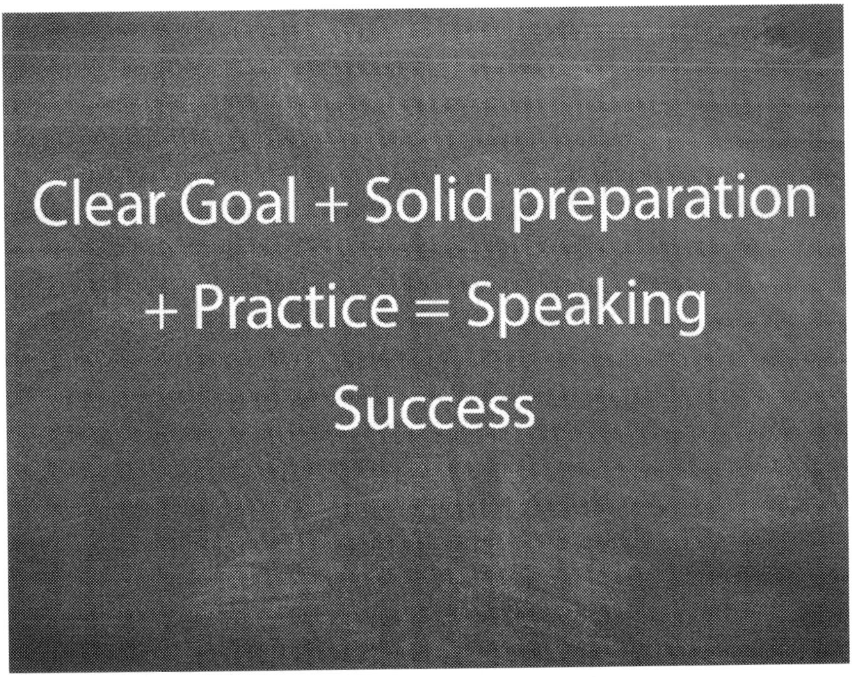
Clear Goal + Solid preparation
+ Practice = Speaking
Success

EVALUATION

Constructive feedback is essential to the professional and personal growth of every speaker.

The best evaluations are a combination of praise, areas for improvement, and specific suggestions. All three elements are essential, but can be mixed in numerous ways. Start your Evaluation by using the sandwich method by describing the strong points of the speech, areas for improvement and specific suggestions and wrap up with praise again. Promote self-esteem by sharing positive reinforcement when improvements occur; make sure your praise is honest and sincere and your evaluation end on a positive note.

Communication is a two-way process. Receivers don't just absorb the message like sponges' they respond to them. The discernible response of the listeners to sender's messages is called evaluation or feedback. Evaluation or Feedback can be in verbal or non-verbal form. This is the most important part of communication that completes the entire loop.

Obtaining good Evaluation is important and vital, provided that the evaluation is honest, fair and supportive. Demonstrate your interest in both the speech and in the speaker's ability to grow and improve. You are helping the speaker to be more effective and improve their speaking skills and abilities. The speaker becomes aware of both their strengths and areas for improvement. Treat novice speakers with extra care. Be a little more encouraging and a little less critical, particularly if they exhibit a high level of speaking fear. Compliment them on tackling and conquering their fear. Reassure them that they aren't as bad as they imagine it to be and overcome their fear. Be supportive.

Studies have shown that specific praise is much more encouraging than generic praise. This applies to criticism as well. Specific feedback (positive or negative) is more meaningful than generic feedback and specific suggestions for improvement. Personalize your language and put yourself in the speaker's shoes before giving an evaluation. Avoid phrases like "you didn't" or "you should have…"

Stimulate improvement with helpful words, such as

"I believe…"

"My reaction was…"

I "suggest"

Evaluate the speech, not the person. Your main goal is to support and encourage, while offering at least one actionable suggestion for improvement. Watch for symptoms of fear or insecurity. Empathize with the speaker's desire to learn and become a better presenter.

THE ART OF HANDLING QUESTIONS

"Teaching is the Art of asking questions"
Socrates)

Dealing with questions in a presentation is a skill which everyone should master. The only way to know that your participants truly understand what you are saying is the acid test or measurement as to whether you are well equipped with sound knowledge of the subject matter and your participants understand what you are saying. The Q&A in public speaking and business presentations is a great way to engage your audience and a great opportunity to be inclusive with other ideas and other points of view.

The traditional place where questions are asked is after the presentation has completed. This is certainly easier for the speaker and perhaps also for most of the audience for whom breaking the flow of learning can be very disrupting.

Another advantage of taking questions at the end is that you can close the talk at the allotted time by not taking any more questions ('Sorry, we've run out of time'). It is common to allow between five to twenty minutes for questions, depending on the talk duration and situation, and sometimes more (such as when your talk is simply to spur a debate).

A potentially more powerful method is to allow people to ask questions on the spot. To do this requires a more assured and confident speaker who can smoothly answer questions and then continue, unruffled, with the talk.

The problem with ad-hoc questions is that they can eat into time in an unpredictable manner. Again, a more comfortable Speaker will manage questioners so they do not take too much time and then change their presentation so that it still flows and completes well on time.

Handling Question and Answer Sessions

Handling the Question and Answer Sessions affects the total impact of a Presentation. When you are asked a question, there are a couple of rules that many speakers forget but which are absolutely critical.

1.   Hear the question

First, listen intently to the questioner. Hear all of their words. Watch their body language. Hear the intent and emotion. If you do not understand what they say, you will have to ask them to repeat themselves, though as this is embarrassing for you and especially them it is best avoided.

2.   Repeat the question

The next step is as important as it is simple: repeat the question and the questioner must speak through a microphone, many other people may not have heard the question, which will make your answer meaningless to them.

Repeating the question also lets you check that you have heard them correctly. This is often best done paraphrasing the question and perhaps simplifying it (many people use a lot of words to ask a simple question).

3.   When you do not know the Answer

If you do not know the answer, then do not try to bluster and fake an authoritative answer. One way of handling this is to bounce it back to the audience, asking what they think about the question and seeking their help in developing a good answer. This method cannot be used with all questions of course, but it can be a life-saver when you are stuck.

4. Admit you don't know but promise to find out the answer?

This is an acceptable way to handle the situation but be sure that you do indeed follow up with an answer and that you do so in a timely manner. Another, simpler approach is simply to say that it is a good answer but you cannot do it justice here. You can, if appropriate, promise to research further and come back with an answer at a later date.

5. Throw the question to the Audience?

I believe this is the best of the three choices. It engages the audience and often provides an insightful discussion. You can say something to the effect of "That's a great question. I don't have an answer. What do you the rest of you think? How would you handle this?" I sometimes throw questions to the audience even when I do know the answer just to see what others think. "I have an idea but I'd really like to hear what everyone else thinks."

- *Prime the Pump!*
  - o People are often reluctant to be the first to ask a question. *Prime the Pump* by *planting* a question with an audience member *before* you present.
  - o *You* ask the first question. This can be done in several ways.
  - o Say, "*I'll* ask the first question. One of the questions I'm typically asked is. . ."
  - o In your **Opening**, tell the audience that *you* will start the Q&A by *asking for a take-away* from several audience participants. (You might want to *plant* this answer, or you might ask them to *write* their *take-away* and call on the person you observed doing the most writing.)

ROYALE PREMIER TOASTMASTERS CLUB

Royal Premier Toastmasters Club, Kuala Lumpur was established on January 11, 2018 by Rita Corray.

The President's Message

It is my privilege to be the Founder and President of Royal Premier Toastmasters and in this special year in which we celebrate our 1st Anniversary. It gives me tremendous joy to welcome you to learn from each other and to celebrate our Toastmasters journey during the past 18 months. On behalf of the Club, I bring you warm wishes and felicitous greetings.

Our club provides a pleasant, calm, and encouraging environment where we learn to step out of our comfort zones and start our own exciting journey of Self-Discovery. Personally, I believe we all need to recognize each individual character, potential and help her/him to grow and develop through active involvement in the club meetings.

We, at Royal Premier Toastmasters is like a BIG family, enjoying our regular meetings, social events, with other club members while developing ourselves. I would like to express my heartfelt thanks to all Chartered Members Gerard Peter, Kevin Wu, Wong Chee Jun,Jeselin and Thana.

Without the contribution from our valued members, current and past officers of this club, Royale Premier Toastmasters Club would not have been a successful club. Therefore, my sincere and heartfelt thanks goes to all members (current and past) and all Exco Officers (current and past) who dedicated their time, support and energy towards the success of Royal Premier Toastmasters.

I wish our club would develop every day by serving all our members. I wish my club would be the best club in the world for our members. Please come and join with us. WE ARE THE BEST.

Our Club's Meeting
On every 1 & 3ᵗʰ Thursday of the month!
Time: 7.00 p.m. – 9.00 p.m.
Venue: Royal Selangor Club at Dataran Merdeka
Click to know more about Toastmasters International.
https//www:.facebook.com/Royale Premier Toastmasters Club

Our Venue: Royal Selangor Club at Dataran Merdeka

Royal Premier Toastmasters Club is a non-profit educational organization, running educational programs according to the Toastmasters International, helping people to do better in Communication and Leadership Skills. We meet every 1st and 3rd Thursdays of the Month.

We run programs from Toastmasters International and focus on Communication and Leadership Skills. Begin your toastmasters journey with us; Here we learn, and practise together. Be part of Toastmasters program running world wide!

A Toastmasters club is nothing fancy or prestigious. It's merely a place where people from all walks of life come together for different purposes, whether to improve their Communication Skills, Leadership Skills or even to find some activity by socializing and having fun.

Mission: To help men and women learn the arts of speaking, listening, and thinking – vital skills that promote self-actualization, enhance leadership potential, foster human understanding, and contribute to the betterment of mankind.

EARNING MY DISTINGUISHED TOASTMASTERS AWARD

By Rita Corray, DTM, District 51, President of Royale Premier Toastmasters Club

> "A journey of a thousand miles begins with a single step."
> ~ Confucius

The Distinguished Toastmaster (DTM) award represents the highest level of educational achievement in Toastmasters As I think about my Toastmasters journey, it was the encouragement and motivation of a single friend; in my case, a very good friend, who worked with me in the same office. He came to me one day, very excited, and told me all about Toastmasters and about this great opportunity to improve our Speaking Skills. "It's great! You get to give prepared speeches, hear evaluations of what you did, and even learn to speak off the cuff to a question given on the spot! You'll love it!!" Toastmasters.

It had taken 20 years for me to reach this destination called – Distinguished Toastmaster.(DTM). So many lovely people had contributed and helped me along in my long journey.

Many Senior Toastmasters including DTM Cyril Jones, DTM Andal Krishnan, DTM Victor Ong, Kevin Wu , were all passionately supporting me to achieve my DTM Dream. Thank you, folks. You are the reason for my meaningful journey of being an effective Speaker.

I believe Toastmasters is all about peer learning, friendship, mutual support and growing together. My sincere Gratitude and Thanks to everyone who contributed to my Toastmasters Journey. Thank you so very much.

I never even remotely imagined that I will become a full-time Professional Speaker and Trainer in my life. I am grateful that I picked a large part of these skills from Toastmasters.

I am always indebted to this stupendous organization **Toastmasters –**

"Where Leaders Are Made".

It has helped me learn the arts of Speaking, Listening, and Thinking — vital skills that promote self-actualization, enhance leadership potential, foster human understanding, and contribute to the betterment of mankind.

Toastmasters is an organization that enables members to improve communication skills in a safe, encouraging, supportive environment.

People are often confused by the name "Toastmasters." Some think it's about learning how to give toasts at events. A few even think the organization has something to do with making toast.

If the name "Toastmasters" sounds old-fashioned, it could be because the organization's roots go back to 1924 when Ralph C. Smedley held the first meeting of what would eventually become Toastmasters International.

THE STORY OF RUTH HO

How I had motivated and inspired my daughter Ruth Ho be a Public Speaker in the Media World

She started her journey in Public Speaking at a very young age. I started to organize Public Speaking Workshops for Children and Ruth was involved by playing a role of Master of Ceremony or by giving a speech. I had always believed that Public Speaking is a skill that is acquired through practice and I had exposed her to a lot of opportunities that was available in Public Speaking. In her lifelong journey of learning Public Speaking has changed her life quite a bit. She took every opportunity to take part in debates and Public Speaking activities in her school or in Children's or Teen's activities outside school.

I have planted the seeds in her, nurtured it and had hoped and dreamed that one day it will blossom into a beautiful flower or fruit. The greatest gift that I am able to give her and my children are the skills and values that I have taught them. Success is no accident. Hard work, Perseverance and Sacrifices are some of the attributes needed to succeed.

Sowing also the Spiritual things, the Seeds of Life.

1 Cor. 9:11 says, *We have sown to you the spiritual things.* What we sow into others are not doctrines or teachings but spiritual seeds, containers of life. **Sowing the Seeds Of Life** – the containers of life – into others is a matter of life, a matter of imparting life into others.

What Has Public Speaking Skills Done To Ruth Ho

Today, Ruth is 24 years old

Ruth Ho is a Malaysian-born NTV7 News Anchor, FLYFM Radio Announcer, Professional Emcee and Television Sports Presenter who is well experienced in the industry. Having been in the Media Industry for 7 years ranging from Production, Journalism, Radio and TV, Ruth Ho had decided to embark on her journey by extending her Marketing and Communication Skills by working in the Management Consulting world in an International Company in Malaysia.

Given the opportunity of working in Media and in a professional firm, it has given her the key skills in adapting to different environments, time management and most importantly working in a professional and fast-paced work environment. She believes that the key in succeeding in both industries is to never rest on your laurels but treat each day as a new learning opportunity.

Congratulations to your success. The proudest moment as a parent is to see your child succeed I want to let the world know that I am so proud of my daughter I want to shout it from the rooftop.

Keep it up. It is your reward for all the hard work you put in. Enjoy every moment of it. It is a success, you truly deserve. It is an achievement you have truly worked hard and earned. I congratulate you on your success and wish you all the best for all your future undertakings.

There is only one thing that makes a dream impossible to achieve: the fear of failure.

CORPORATE TRAINING PROGRAMMES

BY RITA CORRAY AND HER TEAM OF TRAINERS

- ☐ *Impactful Public Speaking Skills*
- ☐ *Train the Trainers*
- ☐ *Business Communication Skills Workshop*
- ☐ *Clerical Development Programs*
- ☐ *Office Administrative Skills Workshop*
- ☐ *English Language Workshops*
- ☐ *Phone Power/Telephone Courtesy*
- ☐ *Business Writing Skills Workshop*

LIST OF COMPANIES TRAINING HAD BEEN CONDUCTED

1. Bank Negara
2. IBM
3. MARA
4. Petronas
5. GD Express
6. Astro
7. Perodua
8. Allianz General Insurance
9. Affin Bank Berhad
10. Affin General Insurance
11. Texas Instrument
12. Samsung
13. Nationwide Courier Service
14. MAA General Assurance
15. HSBC Bank
16. CIMB Bank
17. Proton Holding
18. Bank Pembanguan
19. UTAR
20. Cubic Electronics
21. DRB Hicom
22. Sabah Bank
23. Sunway University (Teaching English on a regular basis).

24. **Hitachi**
25. **First Choice Suppermarket**
26. **Damino Plaza**
27. **Honda – Malacca**

PICTURES OF MY CORPORATE TRAINING

Corporate Training in Sibu

Our Team

Training in Kuching

Using Visual Aids

At a Toastmasters Meeting

Develop the skills needed to Present Effectively

Our Training provides courses for effective Presentation Skills, and our modules provide the knowledge and tactics that empower you to communicate confidently and competently to cater to all types of audiences. View the unique and effective modules we offer to learn more about immediately delivering effective presentations.

For further information, please

contact Rita Corray for any In House Training at

rita@candlelight-training.com
Visit our website at www.candlelight-training/vl.
Tel: 60+ 0172001277

<u>CONCLUSION</u>

"Learning is a Treasure". It is no secret. The author of this book hope that readers will find the chapters in this book useful in developing their own communication competences. Whether you are new to giving presentations, or a more experienced speaker, it is important to remember that the best way to improve your public speaking skills is through preparation and practice. Although it may take time to learn effective speaking skills, the effort is well worth the benefits you will reap in your personal, professional, and public life. It is definitely very important to know that everyone can learn and master the art of Presentation.

Identify opportunities to practice and look for avenues for feedback throughout the process. Self-monitoring and review is also helpful to grade your progress.

Learning to communicate and speak effectively is a lifelong journey. It should be a habit we should all develop.

This book is a must-read if you want to move your career to the next level. The author brings all her experience as a Trainer, Coach and a Writer and has designed this book specially for anyone who aspires to be a great Speaker. My Toastmasters journey had helped me tremendously. I no longer stay in the shadows or hide away but have moved to the center stage of my life. It is never too late to stretch your winds and take flight. Stepping out of my comfort zone and my shelf I feel ready to step out into the world and share my inspiration. It has been a truly amazing journey.

So Fulfilling and Purposeful.

William Hung wrote "If I could live my life with courage, or live my life in fear and hope that people would forget about me" We can choose to take the high road – we can be positive despite negative things happening around us.

Finally, to conclude I would like to stress that to develop Public Speaking and Communication Skills, it includes many factors such as the way we respond to the person we are speaking to, our body gestures, our Facial Expression, Eye Contact, Pitch, Intonation, Tone of our Voice and Pronunciation.

I would like to thank all those who had made a difference in my life and contributed to where I am today especially those who left footprints in my life. Our Tagline *"To Be Different"*

APPENDIX 1

WHERE DO YOU STAND AS A SPEAKER?

Name of Person :

Dept :

Job Title :

The following questions will help you discover your present speaking abilities. During the Workshop you will be able to review your own progress.

Do you......   <u>Yes</u>   <u>No</u>

➤ Feel comfortable talking to other people?   _____ _____

➤ Have trouble explaining your views or ideas   _____ _____

➤ Have nervous habits when you speak, such as _____ _____
Saying "uh", "um", "ok", "and", or fumbling
with buttons or clothing, or jiggling change
in your pocket?

➤ Consider your audience's needs and interests _____ _____
when preparing a presentation?

➤ Plan your presentations with a clear purpose _____ _____
or goal in mind.

➤ Appear to be natural and sincere when speaking? _____ _____

➤ Listen carefully and analytically to others?   _____ _____

➤ Feel comfortable receiving feedback from others? _____ _____

➤ Offer feedback in a positive way that doesn't _____ _____
cause others pain or embarrassment?

➤ Do you often do presentations?   _____ _____

What do you hope to achieve during the two days' Workshop

APPENDIX 2

SPEECH EVALUATION FORM

Name of Speaker   :

Subject   :

Date   :

Please complete the Evaluation Form by rating the Speech using the Scale Below:

1. Must Improve   2. Should Improve   3. Satisfactory
4. About Average   5. Excellent

2.

NO	CATEGORY	RATING
1.	Manner – (Confident, Sincere)	
2.	Preparation And Content	
3.	Organization of Speech – logical flow, Intro, Body and Conclusion	
4.	Voice	
5.	Words – Language	
6.	Body Language	
7.	Value of Speech	
8.	Overall Rating	

APPENDIX 3

My Achievements in my Public Speaking Journey

FOR FURTHER READING:

https://webcache.googleusercontent.com/search?q=cache:3ojEGXjbdRcJ:https://www.slideshare.net/marydelle/four-types-of-public-speaking+&cd=12&hl=en&ct=clnk&gl=ph

https://business.tutsplus.com/tutorials/what-is-public-speaking--cms-31255

https://publicspeakingpower.com/why-is-public-speaking-important/

http://www.geraldgillis.com/importance-speaking-skills/

https://www.speechmastery.com/types-of-public-speaking.html

https://www.slidecow.com/blog/different-types-public-speaking/

http://www.lindsaycook.net/articles/finding-your-passion/

https://courses.lumenlearning.com/boundless-communications/chapter/steps-of-preparing-a-speech/

https://www.coursehero.com/file/p31l3n9/The-Conclusion-Signal-the-end-of-the-speech-Crescendo-ending-a-conclusion-in/

https://hbr.org/2013/06/how-to-give-a-killer-presentation

https://www.genardmethod.com/blog/bid/144247/
the-5-key-body-language-techniques-of-public-speaking

https://junior-broker.com/life/careers/list-of-body-language/

https://www.wikihow.com/Develop-a-Perfect-Speaking-Voice

https://www.verywellmind.com/public-speaking-skills-3024308

https://www.inter-activ.co.uk/presentation-skills/
speaking-off-the-cuff/

https://www.essentiallifeskills.net/develop-good-habits.html

https://drmichellemazur.com/2013/02/7-habits-of-highly-successful-
speakers.html

https://malangtmc.wordpress.com/evaluator/

http://changingminds.org/techniques/speaking/speaking_tips/
handling_questions.htm

Printed in the United States
By Bookmasters